Mieshu's and Moeka's Misery

Mary Therese Pardinek

DEDICATION

Into everyone's life a little rain must fall. Farmers always desire rain, during a drought, when their crops need water. Nevertheless, for most, one appreciates rays of sunshine that brightly pierce through and replace away dark depressing tear filled clouds. Friends and family too can provide the drought, rain clouds, and sunshine in one's life. Personal rejection occurs like a drought when one's emotional needs remain unfulfilled. Non- beneficial rain clouds develop when problems bring tears. Moreover, sunshine results when sincere offered support is uplifting and welcomed during one's times of need. Kelly is one of those friends who brought sunshine during recent times into this author's drought ridden and cloud filled experience. Thank you for your words of encouragement and support. They have made a big difference in keeping me on track. Your assistance has also motivated me to further pursue, accept, and develop my creative needs. Thank you my friend.

Mieshu's

and

Moeka's Misery

*A Poem —About Relationships,
Emotional Baggage,
Divorce, and a Lack of Integrity.*

Contents

DESIRES

▾

Mieshu and Moeka were young –in thought and at heart.

They wanted much from life, to live it in full and enjoy each part.

They lived in neighboring communities that seemed more like a crowded city.

Urban advantages allowed someone to become anyone believed as his or her duty.

✦

Moeka dreamed a future of wealth and happiness.

She took steps necessary to realize her fabulousness.

▪

Mieshu desired a life of power and fame.

He took as many short cuts possible and did not worry about ruining his name.

It would take many years to determine if their dreams would eventually become true.

Only time and the results of many decisions would reveal life's outcome for these two.

Moeka loved and desired to learn.

She figured a good education would help the finances she wanted to earn.

She was good at study and obtained as much knowledge as one could possibly desire.

She went to college and learned how to be an excellent engineer a company would hire.

Her education provided the resources for her success.

She performed her duties well and worked to better her finances by settling for nothing less.

She had become the woman she wanted and desired.

However, her prosperity left her feeling lonely, sad, and emotionally tired.

Mieshu remained active and physical in his pursuits.

He worked as a contractor and learned to build for different client recruits.

He made good money but failed to save.

However, each passing day made him feel more like a financial looser and laboring slave.

Mieshu spent his time and energy spending the little money that seemed to remain.

Yet he still dreamed of power and fame.

RELATIONSHIPS

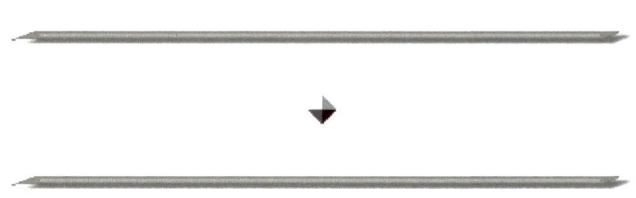

Mieshu and Moeka met each other one summer day.

He sought her attention so the two could play.

Moeka had found a mate to share her time.

Mieshu had found a woman with money that he would call mine.

◆

The two seemed to fill the voids the other might lack.

If only either could know their future and the problems, they would need to attack.

■

Moeka desired a companion with whom she felt comfortable.

Little did she know she would further experience traumas that previously caused her much trouble?

Moeka unwittingly chose a man with a trait similar to her mother.

However, she was unaware of the emotional baggage deep within her.

Moeka believed her mother's words of love were true.

Unfortunately, regular despondent actions bestowed upon Moeka caused her to feel sad and blue.

Moeka conditioned herself to endorse words rather than opposing action.

The truth of one's love results in kindness and satisfaction.

Moeka had no better gauge from which to have judged,

Than to confuse words given as love rather than understand the selfishness, her mother begrudged.

Throughout Moeka's childhood, her father also remained aloof and showed her little interest.

He had better things to do rather than spend time and affections that children desire their parents invest.

Mieshu too may have chosen a woman with similar traits he experienced while parented.

Psychology suggests dysfunctional relationships continue because they remain comfortably warranted.

MARRIAGE

Both should have run as far
from each other and
considered it best.

Nevertheless, they united for
better or worse and put their
characters to test.

Moeka had made decisions that were good for her career.

Mieshu had only pursued passing frivolities that at the time he felt dear.

✦

The two had the strengths of each now combined into one.

They could blend their talents and preferably make life more enjoyable and fun.

✦

However, the way they managed and respected their

marriage vows was sad
indeed.

Mieshu and Moeka seemed to
focus their energy and time
purely on matters of greed.

It took only seven years to see
their marriage fully end.

However, it would take
decades for the pain and their
emotional scares to mend.

Both started their relationship with the best of intentions and a desire to bond their hearts.

It was a shame that neither would complement the others' abandoned character parts.

◆

Moeka was overjoyed she had found a companion and that was all she wanted.

But, her husband's dreams would make her own needs feel most taunted.

✚

Mieshu was intelligent and very smart.

Surely, he was someone a woman of knowledge could love and give her heart.

She initially enjoyed him very much.

They would spend days upon days of happiness and loving touch.

Mieshu also appreciated Moeka's business perception and other such skills.

It seemed they would live happily ever after despite the world's ills.

DISAGREEMENTS

✦

However soon after their "I do's", all hopes changed into disaster.

If the two of them did not suffer so much, their situation would bring laughter.

The more they tried to make their perfect life the further away it would slip.

It was much like each was doing their part to add flood waves to a sinking ship.

◈

Their marriage deterioration started slow to progress.

At first, there were disagreements then a retrieve from the stress.

They were not able to join their efforts to build a happy marriage together.

Their marital dreams were instead in opposition and at expense of each other.

Moeka desired to live financially within their means.

Mieshu desired to enjoy every enticement as if he were king.

31

In addition, Mieshu desired to be the head of their household and financial master.

Moeka seemed happy just finding someone who loved her even if that love was a total disaster.

Their discord compounded one frustration upon another.

Into an abyss of chaos, they had fallen with too many problems to smother.

EFFORTS

↓

In a union determined to last.

They started a business to correct their past.

◆

The business provided each with a need to be.

For better or worse, the result was a terrible reality.

When compared to their miserable marriage that showed much distress.

Their business by contrast was a huge success.

It triumphed in profits from marketing and growth.

However, misuse of wealth caused unhappiness and

deterioration of character for both.

Strangely, neither understood the dilemma they would eventually concede.

The business took all their effort and energy to make it succeed.

It was as if they became unknown.

Living and working together
yet separate islands unto each
other sewn.

Now harbored between them were emotional poverty, anger and guilt.

Instead of joy, stagnation, inertia, a lack of love felt.

Their marriage was not one that most dreams and fairytales told.

It was a master of deception that began to unravel and unfold.

Mieshu found it difficult to accept himself for him.

He would tell lies to Moeka and others on a whim.

He claimed his love for her many times over in whole and by fractions.

Yet his words of love would not live up to any of his actions.

His behavior exposed the real motives from this youth.

Sadly however Moeka
believed his words of lies and
thought of them beautiful
truth.

Deep down she knew there
were problems that should not
be.

However, she refused to open
her eyes fully to better see.

Her ears provided the rationalization for what her eyes did not want to believe.

Her husband was a louse and that fact she could not accept or ably conceive.

■

DIVORCE

✦

Eventually Moeka avoided her feelings through emotional withdrawal.

She refused to react to Mieshu's many actions that caused her appall.

✤

She found evidence that her husband's love was unsound.

The desire she needed to fight for her marriage was to be unfound.

Mieshu entangled himself in a romance with another.

She was a woman who was old enough to be Mieshu's mother.

The woman also wanted wealth that results from power and fame.

Mieshu had found a new companion and told her many lies in order to make his claim.

■

A fraudulent and untrustworthy relationship prevailed.

For these two also became financially derailed.

@

No matter how now unwilling,
Mieshu and Moeka once did
care.

Yet their marriage was long
past any point of repair.

It resulted in selfishness,
deception, and an expensive
affair.

Moeka had no choice, but to
sink further into despair.

Mieshu thought he could start over with the other woman instead.

Leaving Moeka, and wishing her, dead.

■

It is all very sad but it is what it is.

Their divorce decree granted Mieshu possessions of Moeka also as his.

When two people choose money over other values that also are dear,

Life shows an outcome, which offers very little about which to cheer.

⊹

Their marriage was unsuited and disastrous for each.

Doom resulted from dishonesty and intentional deceit.

⊹

Instead of a happy resolve, Moeka felt imprisoned by her spouse she once desired to love and cherish.

When one partner is foreign to integrity there is no common ground and loving affections eventually perish.

◈

Integrity and honesty go hand in hand.

Deceit and dishonesty will undermine any faithful stand.

▪

Nevertheless, try to make it work they did, one for convenience and comfort, the other for love and devotion.

Only their business absorbed the fruits of their affections and emotion.

Now both their business and marriage are gone.

Only turmoil and grief remain as their collective pawn.

Money and marriage go side
by side.

Yet, to care about only one
and not the other makes for an
unstable ride.

■

It could have been that these
two would gain.

If only their focus was to
complement the inner desires
of each that now caused such
disdain.

@

It takes both spouses to make a marriage relationship work and keep it well.

When one only takes and the other just gives, their union becomes a real hell.

Mieshu lacked integrity to make him whole.

In addition, Moeka thought any husband would support her lonely soul.

Both suffered because their union was not sound.

Their differing characters destroyed the marital essence once thought they found.

●

Neither party benefited from this seven-year union.

It will take more years total to undo the negativities absorbed and restore them to their origin.

■

Everyone lost who knew these parties involved.

Is not life about going forward, growing better, stronger and more evolved?

Not with the problems that surfaced and were briefly described herein.

When dealing with matters of the heart, brokenness is the worst of all possible sin.

So learn that life is about the decisions we make.

For better or worse, our lives are at stake.

❀

Live up to the responsibilities that make us whole.

Avoid the dilemmas' that can eventually steal our soul.

▪

Keep us sound to the right principles at hand.

Make certain our well-beings strengthen by the values for which we stand.

■

Learn to love and appreciate life.

Without care and respect, money can mean nothing but a journey full of strife.

INTEGRITY

→

Integrity is a most personal possession.

Those that have integrity know it, and so do all others that meet those of integrity.

Those that lack integrity can fool some of the people some of the time. They can even fool themselves, but eventually all know they lack it.

Integrity is available to anyone willing to possess it.

Nevertheless, for many, it does not come easily, and those that lack integrity have a very difficult time living a content life.

For this story, and many others,

…There is

No End

—Life and its progression of events
continue.

www.wonderfulmanuscripts.com